MYSTERY!
MYSTERY!
MYSTERY!

Missing!

Katie Dicker

A+

Smart Apple Media

Published by Smart Apple Media,
an imprint of Black Rabbit Books
P.O. Box 3263, Mankato, Minnesota, 56002
www.blackrabbitbooks.com

Designed by Hel James
Edited by Mary-Jane Wilkins

Cataloging-in-Publication Data is available from the Library of Congress

ISBN 978-1-62588-201-1

Photo acknowledgements
title page Özer Öner, pages 2-3 iStock/Thinkstock, 4 straga/
Shutterstock; 5, 8, 9 iStock/Thinkstock; 13 Baloncici/Shutterstock;
14 Özer Öner, 15 LFink/both Shutterstock; 16, 18 iStock/Thinkstock;
19 Thomas Barrat/Shutterstock; 20-21 iStock/Thinkstock; 20 Mary
Frances Howard/Powers Photos; 24 Özer Öner
Cover iurii/Shutterstock

Artwork Q2A Media Art Bank

Printed in China

DAD0054
032014
9 8 7 6 5 4 3 2 1

Contents

Lost and Found

*A man goes missing and the police are trying to find him. He seems to have **vanished**— where can he be? People go missing all the time. Some turn up and others are found, but a few are lost forever.*

Last Run

*In a famous **legend**, James Worson, a shoemaker from Leamington Spa, UK, bet his friends he could run all the way to Coventry. During the eight mile (14 km) run in 1873, James was said to stumble and fall "with a terrible cry." He vanished and was never seen again.*

Strange Stories

In Vermont in 1950, eight-year-old Paul Jepson disappeared from a farm. Paul's mother left her son playing near a pig pen while she looked after the animals. When she returned, Paul was missing. He was never found.

Some people go missing because they run away, but others may have been taken.

Disappearing Act

In another story, Tennessee farmer David Lang was walking across a field in 1880 when he disappeared in front of his wife, children, and a local judge passing by. A few months later, David's children found a circle of yellow grass where their dad had disappeared. But where had David gone?

Secrets at Sea

Some people mysteriously vanish without trace at sea. No remains are found beneath the deep water, and no wreckage is discovered floating on the waves.

Final Voyage

In 1872, a ship called the Mary Celeste set sail from New York to Genoa in Italy. Later, she was seen drifting near the coast of Portugal. A passing ship went to investigate, but no one was found on board. The ten passengers had completely disappeared!

Gathering Evidence

The ship's lifeboat was missing, but there was food and water on board. The **logbook** had no reports of danger. Did the lifeboat sink, or did the passengers land on a nearby island? Perhaps a sea creature ate them all.

Captain Briggs and his family and crew vanished from the Mary Celeste in 1872.

Abandoned Ship

Less than ten years after the Mary Celeste, another crew disappeared at sea. The Ellen Austin was sailing near the island of Bermuda when her captain saw a drifting ship. He sent six sailors to investigate. There was no one on board—it was like a ghost ship! Captain Baker asked the sailors to take the ship to shore.

Missing in the Mist

The two ships sailed together, but as night fell, a thick fog filled the air. In the darkness, Captain Baker lost sight of the other ship.

No Trace

When daylight came, the mist lifted, but the ghost ship had completely disappeared! The Ellen Austin's crew searched in vain; the mystery ship and the sailors were never seen again.

The ghost ship and its crew of sailors vanished without trace.

Last Journey

At the end of the 19th century, another famous ship disappeared. The Marlborough set sail from New Zealand to London in 1890 with 30 passengers. A passing ship saw it two days later, but it was never seen again. People thought that the Marlborough had sunk after hitting an iceberg.

MARLBOROUGH

Bones on Board

More than 20 years later, a ship sailing near **Cape Horn** *in South America saw another ship drifting nearby. A search party went to investigate. To their horror, they found a skeleton on deck. There were other remains on board. How did the* Marlborough *survive the sea's stormy conditions for more than two decades? Why was it not discovered before, and what happened to the crew?*

Strange Stories

In 1979, five men went missing at sea. During a fishing trip near the Hawaiian island of Maui, their boat—the *Sarah Joe*—vanished after a storm and the men were feared drowned. Nine years later, parts of their boat were found on an island 2,000 miles (3,220 km) away, along with the bones of one of the crew in an unmarked grave. No one knows what happened or how the body was buried.

The Bermuda Triangle

If you're going on a journey, beware of the Bermuda Triangle! Many passing ships and planes have gone missing from this area, never to be seen again.

Coal Carrier

In 1918, a huge **cargo** ship called the Cyclops was carrying coal between America and Brazil. On its return journey through the Bermuda Triangle, it vanished without trace. All 306 people on board also disappeared...

Lost Contact

More recently, in 1992, Michael Plant set sail in his boat Coyote. *When he reached the Bermuda Triangle, he reported something strange. Then he lost both electrical power and radio contact. Months later, Michael's boat was found upside down some miles away. His body was never found.*

Michael Plant disappeared after losing radio contact. No one knows what happened to him.

Final Flights

Planes, as well as ships, have gone missing from the Bermuda Triangle. In 1945, six planes disappeared as they flew overhead. Five US army planes were training in the area, and another flew by in the search for **survivors**.

Lost Bearings

Charles Taylor was the army officer in charge that day. After he'd been flying for an hour, his **compass** stopped working and he lost his way. The weather grew worse and it was hard to see. Taylor told the pilots to fly east, but the planes were running out of fuel and it was getting dark.

The planes lost their way as they flew over the ocean.

Search Party

Shortly after 7p.m., the planes lost radio contact. A rescue operation searched night and day, but no planes could be found. One of the search planes also went missing. That day, 27 men may have lost their lives.

The remains of the planes have never been found.

Vanishing Act

*Perhaps the mystery of the Bermuda Triangle is linked to **aliens** and **UFOs**. Some people blame strange disappearances on creatures from outer space. What do you think?*

Sleepwalking?

In 1959, Bruce Campbell was staying in a hotel in Jacksonville, Illinois, with his wife. During the night, Bruce disappeared. When his wife woke up, she found the bed next to her empty. Bruce's belongings—wallet, money, shoes, glasses, keys, and clothes—were still there. Only his pajamas were missing.

If Bruce ran away, why did he leave all his personal belongings behind?

Mystery Man

For many weeks, police searched for Bruce. They offered a reward for his recovery, but Bruce and his green pajamas seemed to have vanished from the face of the Earth. Did he run away or get lost? Or perhaps he was kidnapped.

Was 57-year-old Bruce Campbell kidnapped by aliens?

Strange Stories

In 1975, Jackson and Martha Wright were driving to New York City and stopped the car to wipe the windshield. Martha went to clean the back window, but when Jackson turned around, his wife had gone. Martha had simply disappeared.

Missing Passenger

Some people disappear in the strangest places. In 1968, Jerrold Potter was on a plane with his wife, flying to Dallas. He went to the restroom, but was never seen again. Cabin staff found the plane's rear door slightly ajar—had Jerrold fallen, or did he jump? There were no witnesses, and there was no reason for Jerrold to throw himself from a plane.

Did 54-year-old Jerrold fall, jump, or was he pushed?

Curious Couple

Edward and Stephania Andrews had left a cocktail party in Chicago, in 1970, when they vanished in their car. As the 62-year-old couple drove away, they caught the attention of the parking attendant —Stephania was crying and Edward scraped the car before driving north on the southbound lane! The couple didn't turn up for work and their home was deserted. They were reported missing, and have not been found to this day.

Strange Stories

In 1949, a man mysteriously vanished from a crowded bus. Mr. Tetford, who lived in Vermont, was on his way home when he disappeared from the vehicle. Witnesses said they saw Tetford sleeping in his seat, but when the bus reached its destination, he had disappeared. His belongings were on the luggage rack and a bus timetable lay open on his seat. No one knows what happened to him.

Police searched the Chicago River, but no trace of the Andrews or their car has ever been found.

Still Searching

Police continue to search for clues to disappearances. In 2007, famous adventurer Steve Fossett disappeared while flying over the Nevada Desert. Although some of his remains were found, the reason for his death is still a mystery.

Record-Breaker

Steve Fossett was known for breaking many world records—such as flying alone around the world in a hot-air balloon. In 2007, he set off in a small plane over the desert and was never seen again.

Steve Fossett was a record-breaking adventurer.

Unsolved Mystery

Steve's disappearance was a mystery for more than a year. Then a hiker in the Sierra Nevada Mountains found his ID cards. A search of the area revealed the wreckage of a burnt-out, crashed plane, and two of Steve's bones. How did such an experienced flier crash in the mountains?

Could the Sierra Nevada Mountains hold more clues to Steve Fossett's death?

Strange Stories

Amelia Earhart was another famous adventurer who went missing. During an attempt to fly around the world in 1937, Amelia and her **navigator** Fred Noonan disappeared over the Pacific Ocean. Despite a massive air and sea search, no trace of Amelia, Fred, or their plane was found. Some think the pair drowned when their plane ran out of fuel and crashed. Others think they may have landed on an island.

Glossary

aliens
Creatures from another planet.

Cape Horn
A rocky headland at the southern tip
of South America, where the seas
are rough and dangerous.

cargo
Goods transported
by road, rail, or sea.

compass
An instrument with
a magnetic needle that
always points north.
Travelers use
a compass to work
out the direction
they are moving in.

legend
An old story that has
been handed down
from the past, which
may or may not be true.

logbook
A written record of a ship's journey.

navigator
Someone who works out the direction in which a ship,
plane, or car should go, using maps and other instruments.

survivors
People who have lived through a terrible accident
or disaster.

UFOs
Unidentified flying objects.

vanished
Disappeared.

Web Sites

www.castleofspirits.com/strangediss.html
Tales of people who have vanished into thin air.

www.bermuda-triangle.org
More mysteries from the Bermuda Triangle.

www.exploringlifesmysteries.com/mysterious-
disappearances
Mysterious disappearances from around the world.

Index